# They Lied
## The REAL Cost of Your Retirement

Adam J Bruno

They Lied

Independently Published

Copyright © 2021 Adam Bruno

Published in the United States of America

210311-01808.1

ISBN: 9798515106188:

No parts of this publication may be reproduced without correct attribution to the author of this book.

For more information on 90-Minute Books including finding out how you can publish your own book, visit 90minutebooks.com or call (863) 318-0464

# Here's What's Inside…

**Introduction** .................................................................. 1

**Chapter One**
**Freedom from Unjust Taxation** ............................... 5

**Chapter Two**
**The True Cost of Your 401(k)** ............................... 16

**Chapter Three**
**The True Cost of Your IRA** .................................... 24

**Chapter Four**
**How the IRS Legally Double Dips on Your IRA** ................................................................... 37

**Chapter Five**
**Freedom from Exorbitant Medicare Surcharges** ................................................................ 45

**Chapter Six**
**IRA and 401(k) Mistakes to Avoid** ....................... 50

**Chapter Seven**
**Exposing the Lie: Success Stories** ........................ 59

**Chapter Eight**
**Questions You Should be Asking** ......................... 63

**Chapter Nine**
**Here's How We Can Help You** .............................. 71

**Exposing the Lie!**
**Discover the "Actual' Cost of Your Retirement** ............................................................... 74

*Investment advisory services are offered through Evolution Wealth Management Inc., an investment advisor registered with the State of Florida. Registration does not imply any level of skill or training. Evolution Wealth Management's unique CRD number is 307644. You can obtain a copy of Evolution Wealth Management's firm brochure (Form ADV Part 2A) free of charge by*
*visiting https://adviserinfo.sec.gov/firm/summary/307644. Evolution Wealth Management offers investment advisory services only where it is appropriately registered or exempt from registration and only after clients have entered into an investment advisory agreement confirming the terms of engagement, and have been provided a copy of the firm's ADV Part 2A. Insurance services provided by Evolution Retirement Services. Any guarantees mentioned are backed by the financial strength, and claims-paying ability of the issuing insurance company and may be subject to restrictions, limitations, or early withdrawal fees, which vary by the issuer. They do not refer in any way to securities or investment advisory products. You should consider the charges, risks, expenses, and investment objectives carefully before entering a contract. This material has been prepared for informational purposes only and should not be construed as a solicitation to effect, or attempt to effect, either transactions in securities or the rendering of personalized investment advice. This material is not intended to provide and should not be relied on for tax, legal, accounting, or other financial advice. Evolution Wealth Management and Evolution Retirement Services do not provide tax, legal, or accounting advice. You should consult your own tax, legal, and accounting advisors before engaging in any transaction. Evolution Wealth Management and Evolution Retirement Services are affiliated entities.*

## Dedication

Arnold Schwarzenegger once said that there is no such thing as someone being "self-made". The people around you are the reason that you find success. The first people I need to thank are my children; Austin, Emeilia, and Maverick. When I look at all of you, I KNOW who I need to be and why I need to never stop growing. You each make me SO proud to be a father every day! My wife Kelly-Ann, none of this is possible without your constant dedication, love, and belief in me. I will never be able to relay in a sentence, paragraph, or entire book, how MUCH I love you. I would also like to thank my Mom, Tina. I love you more infinity!! George, it took me a long time, and I am still learning, but thank you for sticking with me. Becoming a father to a 15-year-old is enough to make you want to jump off a bridge, but you didn't! Andy Burns, there will NEVER be a way to repay your partnership, belief in me or friendship. None of this is possible without you! Patrick Butcher, you recognized all of this in me, even when I didn't. Thank you. You have always been a true friend, and those are hard to come by! Kirk Haldorson, without you, none of this is possible. I have said it before, and I will continue to say it. You are EVERYTHING that I want to be when I grow up!! Thank you for believing in me, and thank you for being the best friend and mentor anyone could ask for. Love you too, Mama Wendy!!!

Chris Sleight, without your partnership and vision, the families that we serve would be lost. You have also been a huge influence on me and showed me the way that I never thought would be possible. Thank you! Bob Grace, thank you for introducing me to a world I had absolutely no idea about. I know we will never be on the best of terms, but I am thankful for you every day. Joel Wheldon, you, my friend, are the greatest speaking and business coach that ANYONE could ask for. You have continued to help me grow and challenged me every step of the way. I will always need it, and you always bring it!! Chris Heerlein, thank you for your friendship, and thank you so much for always being there for me! Mike Carter, you know why. Love you, man!!

Finally, Kurt and Warren, my PARTNERS. I want you to know that NONE of this would have ever happened without you. You are the real Wizards behind the curtain. I know we haven't always seen eye to eye, but there isn't anything that happens in our business without either one of you. Well, maybe not you, Warren, but definitely you, Kurt!......

# Introduction

An important question I hear many times from families I help in retirement is, "Why didn't I know about this?" My main focus for writing this book is to help people understand the difference between Investment Consulting and real Wealth Management. My colleagues from the CEG Group, John Bowen and Russ Allen Prince, have helped me to realize WHY this is such an important distinction.

I HATE the term "Financial Advisor." I have NEVER been able to use that term for myself or others without cringing. The reality is most Financial Advisors are Investment Consultants. *They help their clients by telling them what they should or shouldn't invest in, how to make money, how to accumulate wealth*. This is their job.

There is nothing wrong with this in and of itself. However, when people reach retirement (a point at which they have been told the LIE their entire working life, "It will be easy"), most of the time, they are in for a big surprise. This is because retirement is SO much more than investment consulting. Retirement requires real Wealth Management.

When it comes to Wealth Management, investment consulting is a part of what Wealth Managers do, but Wealth Management is also advanced planning. Advanced planning answers the important questions in retirement, including, "How much money can or should I spend every year? How much in taxes will I pay over my retirement? How much will my beneficiaries pay? How much is Medicare going to cost over my retirement? What does my estate plan look like? Have I protected my assets as much as possible? Are they subject to unjust seizure?"

The last ingredient to true Wealth Management that very few "Financial Advisors" bring to the table is Relationship Management. When it comes to serving their clients, Wealth Managers always have the best choice of professionals working on their teams. That means when you need an estate plan, they have an Estate Planning Attorney in their office and a network of multiple attorneys outside of their office that they have worked with and vetted. They have highly credentialed CPAs and tax professionals in their office and professionals outside of their office whom they have worked with and vetted. Any service you can imagine in retirement they have multiple relationships that have been vetted. This goes far beyond the normal "Financial Advisor," saying that he/she knows someone you can talk to.

Real Wealth Managers already have these "someones" on their team and have used them before as part of the bigger plan being completed for the families they serve. If you are retired or nearing retirement and reading this book, you MUST understand the difference between having a Financial Advisor and having a true Wealth Manager. It is the difference between having an entire TEAM behind you or having one individual helping you with your investments.

After reading this book, I hope you know it is possible to have Roth IRAs that you can move your traditional IRAs into. I also want you to be educated about Medicare Surcharges and how much your retirement will cost you. I want you to stop believing the LIES that other "Financial Advisors" have told you, like, "You don't have to worry about taxes in retirement because your income will be lower." Does this mean that the family is going to spend LESS? Where does the money come from? There are other lies, like, "RMDs are a part of life." They are NOT. There are ways to prevent yourself from EVER having to take an RMD, yet you NEVER hear about it because "Financial Advisors" can't make any additional money from it, and it is MORE WORK for them.

There's no time to waste! Let's look at how your retirement can become a retirement of real significance and abundance.

*Adam*

# Chapter One
# Freedom from Unjust Taxation

When I talk about the concept of unjust taxation, you might automatically think about something like the American Revolution or the Boston Tea Party. The reality is that unjust taxation happens all over the place, and most people don't realize that they're paying too much in retirement. They aren't aware of what the real tax rates and the real dollars look like.

You probably don't understand unjust taxation because you've been paying taxes your entire life in the accumulation phase of your career. When we talk about retirement, you're at a phase where you have to start spending your money to maintain your lifestyle or the distribution phase. You have been told the LIE your entire working career, "Don't worry about when you retire because you're going to be in a lower tax bracket. You're not going to be making as much money." That doesn't necessarily mean that you are going to be spending LESS money.

It's a whole different story in retirement. If you've done a great job saving up a lot of money for retirement, you will have money that you need to start paying yourself, and that money is likely to be taxed because you've probably saved that money in a 401(k) or IRA or another type of Tax-Deferred Vehicle.

Let's use a hypothetical example; a 50-year-old couple who saved up over a million dollars. Their tax bracket will look extremely different from somebody who's in their 60s or 70s at this point. Taxes today are the lowest they've been in over 40 years. Do you really believe that taxes will get lower? That couple is likely to pay much more money to the IRS when they retire than a couple who is in retirement right now or a couple approaching retirement. Taxes are at a discount, right now, today! You aren't aware of these changes because you were not focused on taxes in retirement while you were working and accumulating your wealth. When you turn 65 and retire, or if you've done well and turn 60 and retire, you have a big surprise when you file their taxes, and it sounds something like this: "Wait a minute. My tax bill is HOW MUCH this year!!??"

**Freedom vs. Unjust Taxation**

Unjust taxation is this concept that you're going to pay a lot more money in taxes to the IRS than individuals who haven't saved as much as you. It probably happened to you in your career. The basic concept is that you had a much higher income than everyone else, so you paid more taxes than everyone else. One of the ways this happens during retirement is the RMD trap. This is a set amount of money that you have to take out of Tax-Deferred accounts every year. Well, you don't HAVE to take the money out, but if you don't, you will pay a FIFTY percent tax penalty on the entire amount. Required Minimum Distributions used to have to be taken at age 70 and a half, but now it's 72. When you take it out, you have to ADD this to your income for the year and pay the taxes. This whole concept alone is unjust and backward. Let me tell you why.

I have a few families I represent in Wisconsin and Minnesota. They're farmers, and many of them take advantage of tax-deferred savings such as IRAs and SEP IRAs, where they can put a lot of money away, avoiding the taxes upfront. When we talk about unjust taxation, I explain that putting your money in a 401(k) or an IRA is not the logical way to do things at all. If you're a farmer and you were getting ready for your season when you plant that seed in the ground, would you rather pay the taxes on that seed that you plant in the ground or on the 12 ears of corn that grow from that seed?

Most of us (especially the farmers) would rather pay the tax on the seed that they planted in the ground because it's less tax in the long run. If the seed grows 12 acres of corn, that's your corn. You don't have to pay any taxes on that. We've been trained as a society our entire working career to pay the tax on the corn!! We put $500 a week into our IRA, and Uncle Sam and the IRS say, "Don't worry about paying the taxes on this $500 (the seed). We're going to let that grow tax-free. They're interested in the taxes on what it grows to. They're interested in the taxes on the $500,000 (the corn) it grows to, not the $500 (seed). You, the worker (or the farmer), are doing all the work to grow your corn, and the IRS is receiving a piece of all the work you did!

You've been doing this backward your entire career because you were lied to! It makes more sense to pay the taxes sooner rather than later because "later" usually leads to a situation where the IRS and Uncle Sam win! Remember, the "I" in IRS stands for Immortal, NOT Internal. The IRS is going to outlive all of us. They normally win!

That's an example of unjust taxation. You're paying taxes on all the corn you grow in your field rather than paying the taxes on the seed. Let's face it; if you grow your corn, you're putting the work in. You're watering, and you're planting, you're plowing, your hands are bleeding and blistered, and you're doing all of the work. Imagine somebody coming in after it grows and saying, "Okay, you know what? A third of that corn is mine." They did no work for it. Their hands didn't blister and bleed. It's the same situation with 401(k) and IRA. You got a break on the dollar so they could charge you tax on the $100 bill later on.

**Hidden Surprises**

I've mentioned that one of the biggest surprises I see with families is the amount of taxes that they're going to pay. One of the biggest HIDDEN surprises is what one of my colleagues and mentors in Texas, Chris Heerlein, calls "The Stealth Tax." I've never heard it put better than that. When you retire after doing a great job of saving, and you start paying yourself, you're going to end up paying more for your Medicare costs than your next-door neighbor is. Especially if you already have a high income before you start paying yourself from IRAs. Often, your Medicare costs are three, four, or even five times more than what your neighbor pays just because you did a better job-saving. Often times families that I sit with never even see it or understand it. That's why Chris calls it the stealth tax. Depending on your situation, it could potentially cost families an extra 300 to-500,000 THOUSAND in retirement. We're going to talk about this in-depth in Chapter 5. Still, I think those two things are the biggest surprises because families have been told the LIE their entire careers while they're working, "Don't worry about taxes in retirement."

Eventually, when you retire, if your income doesn't change, you will still need to pay yourself. You have to be able to buy the things you need and maintain your lifestyle. WHERE are all these tax savings that have been promised to you your entire working career? How can you possibly "not worry about it" when you still need to maintain your lifestyle? The reality is that you have never been told about possible tax repercussions in Retirement. Again, if you are working with an investment consultant, a "financial advisor," you are not going to hear about tax strategies or additional costs in retirement. You're only going to hear about how to grow and accumulate your money. I'm not going to judge a financial advisor on whether they do a bad job or do a good job, but the reality is they grow your money, and they make sure you have enough for retirement. It becomes about accumulation and accumulating wealth. There's no focus put on how to spend your money in retirement and how you can spend it in the most tax-efficient way.

We as a society just keep kicking that tax can down the road. To me, that's a prime example of unjust taxation. With the proper planning, most people can enter retirement without any of these issues, without any of these higher tax brackets, Medicare surcharges. It starts when you're working, in your working career. Even if you're retired and reading this book, you still have the opportunity to help your kids, your grandkids, people who need to know, "Hey, I don't want to pay the IRS way more money than everybody else just because I did a good job." Let's get the word out to our families and our loved ones!!!

## My Encouragement to You

The action you can take from this chapter is to make sure you know exactly what your lifestyle looks like. You can't go willy-nilly into your lifestyle in retirement and say, "Okay, I have this much money," because every cent that you take out of 401(k)s and IRAs are going to cost you in taxes. Every cent could contribute to you paying way more in Medicare than you should be.

I've sat with families who want to buy boats. They want to buy cars. They want to buy a vacation home. Where are they going to get the money from that? They're going to get the money from their IRA or their 401(k). When they take that big chunk of money out for that boat or that vacation home or something they want, guess what happens? They pay much more in taxes and medicare surcharges because all of that gets added to their income for that year.

I remember sitting with a couple in 2019 who were concerned enough to come in and talk to me about their situation in Retirement. The gentleman "John" and his wife "Mary", had just purchased a boat and were excited about doing the loop and taking that boat all over the world. They took out $750,000 from an IRA to pay for this boat. John was very happy with himself and the fact that he could afford to do this. This particular couple had over 20 million dollars of investable assets, most of which were in tax-deferred accounts.

I did a lot of listening in this first meeting. He talked a LOT. He told me all about his investments, his style, how well he had done in his career in the market. I noticed that Mary didn't say much. I looked at Mary after John had finally finished his monologue about how great he was, and I asked her, "Mary, why did you come in today?".

Mary told me that they had done well, but she didn't want to see any of the money wasted. She was concerned about the big purchase of the boat, even though they had plenty of money. Mary wanted that money to not be wasted, so whatever was left could go to their children. She had the courage to tell me that she was scared of what she DIDN'T know in retirement.

I looked at John, and I told him to take the boat back. He looked at me, stunned, and said, why would I do that? I informed him that the boat didn't cost him $750,000; it was possible that it could end up, in the long run, costing him double that number. Once I explained the tax bill (which was a ridiculous amount added to his current income), and the increase to his medicare, he realized his mistake. They didn't take the boat back, but we were able to file form SSA44 and save him the huge increase to his Medicare that he would have faced the following year.

# Chapter Two
# The True Cost of Your 401(k)

If you are like most people, you have always done what you've been told and dumped all of your money into a 401(k). The reason that you probably did this was for the tax break or potentially because your employer would match a certain percentage of your contributions.

It's a big mistake to only throw money into your 401(k) for two reasons. The first reason we've already discussed in chapter one. Yes, you're getting a big tax break now on everything that goes into the 401(k), but eventually, you're going to pay taxes on it, likely at a higher tax rate. The second reason; I see families put so much money into a 401(k) because, normally, an employer will match a certain amount that you deposit into your 401(k). What nobody recognizes is that it's a tax break for the employer JUST as much as it is for the employee who's getting that 3% match. So why should you contribute any more than what they are matching you into your 401k? If they only match you 3 percent, it makes very little sense to put any more in. It always seems like it's great that employers match and do these things, but employers are getting taken care of on the tax side of things, too. We don't need to get into that. The problem is that people will put in 10, 15, 20% of their income into their 401(k), and the employer is only matching 5% or 3%.

Why put more into a vehicle that you're eventually going to have to pay taxes on? Also, with your 401(k), your investment options can be very limited based on the plan. I've talked about this idea of Investment Consulting, which is still a portion of what true Wealth Management is. You still have to think about this. With 401(k)s, most of the time, you are very limited as to what your investment options are. They might have a few investment options in each category.

I sat down with a family a couple of months ago. They had retired from a corporation, but while they were working, investment options inside their 401k were very limited. This lead to them investing in a very aggressive manner. They did not have a conservative investment option other than a money market option and a fixed 1 percent option. Can you guess what happened to them? They had to work an extra year after the slight correction last year in the market. They lost so much money because they were invested aggressively due to a lack of options. If they would have had better options, this could have potentially been prevented, and it's entirely possible that they could have retired on time. Now imagine if they kept the money invested that way in the 401k even after they retired! It could end up costing them their entire retirement savings in the event of a major correction.

**The Problem with the Discount**

You get a discounted price, and your money continues to grow. The problem is that, inside the 401(k), you're not worried about capital gains. Once you cash that 401(k) out, you're still responsible for capital gains.

The other thing you need to worry about with 401(k) is the risk-associated limitation investment options. You might only see aggressive investment options heavily tied to the performance of the market. This can be very dangerous later on in life. There's nothing wrong with aggressive investing when you're younger because we have so long to make up for the loss. Later on in life, when you're in your 50s and 60s, and you're getting ready to retire, you can't afford to remain aggressive and have limited investment options. This is the point where you must have conservative, diversified options.

If you don't address this, you might end up in a situation where, all of a sudden, because you were very aggressive in your 401(k), we have a little blip in the market, or there's a major correction, and BOOM, a third or half of the wealth that you've been saving is gone. Normally, that would be okay because you have another 15 or 20 years to rebound and make up for it. However, if you're going to retire in two or three years, there's not enough time to make up the loss. That can be a huge issue. One of the big things that I see is, when people contribute to a 401(k), they think that is their only option, or they have been told that they can't have other accounts, when in fact, they can. You might not have known that there were other ways for you to invest your money when you were working. If you were told this, it was yet another lie.

If you have a 401(k) and the company is only matching your contributions up to 3%, it makes sense for you to go ahead and take the additional 7% that you were going to contribute and put that somewhere else. Let's say you want to contribute 10% of your income towards your retirement. Contribute 3% to your 401k and get your match, then take the additional 7%, pay the tax upfront, and put it into a Roth IRA. It will grow tax-free, and you can take it out tax-free! Pay the taxes upfront and take advantage of the discounted tax environment we are in right now. Everything that you grow inside the Roth from that point forward is tax-free. It belongs to you completely. You don't have to pay taxes to anyone. When you take it out, it's tax-free.

Another big mistake I see with this thought process is sometimes, you don't have any Roth options with your employer, and that's okay.

You don't have to have a Roth account with your employer. You can open your own Roth IRA. Most of the time, when we sit with families in retirement, nobody has ever told them this. That leads to unnecessary costs and taxes in retirement.

We talk about costs; dollars, and cents. Your investments cost you money. There is always a cost associated with investments. You could invest and lose money. You could be paying too much compared to other investment options inside of a 401(k). I have seen it range anywhere from half a percent up to a full percent, depending on what you're investing in inside of your 401(k). Other advisors will tell you, "Well, don't worry about that. It comes out of your performance, so you never see it."
LIES

Listen, if it's money that could have gone into your bank account but didn't, that's money that you're losing! That's money that you're not getting. Do the math! With 401(k)s, you have to remember there is a cost, and don't feel like you have to keep it in that 401(k) because you don't. That's one of the biggest mistakes people have made when they sit down in front of me: "I have this big 401(k). I don't know what to do with it." Well, of course, you don't because they weren't getting the right advice.

**The True Cost of Waiting to Convert**

The true cost of the 401(k) usually comes from a lack of knowledge. For example, families who leave work and have a huge 401(k) plan have no idea that they could have done it in different ways. They feel like they are stuck with what the investment is at this point. This is a lie! They think the costs to move those investments are too high. This is a lie! There are still things that you can do in this situation because these are still funds that the taxes have not been paid on yet. The potential savings could be HUNDREDS of thousands of dollars. You still have the option of CONVERTING to Roth IRA's, but more on this later.

I've dealt with families who had millions of dollars inside of a 401(k) when they retired. Rather than spending that money down normally, with the proper planning, they were able to save themselves SIGNIFICANT amounts of money that would have gone to the IRS. It's a significant savings with the proper planning. The biggest thing you can take from this chapter is that no matter what your situation is right now in retirement, no matter how big that 401(k) is, no matter how big your tax bill is, there's always something that you can do about it with the proper plan. You can still benefit from tax-free growth and tax-free income!

# Chapter Three
# The True Cost of Your IRA

Unfortunately, you may think everything is solved once you move your money over to an IRA. This is another lie. Everything is not solved once the money is rolled into an IRA. From a 50,000-foot view, individual IRAs normally give you many more investment options than a 401(k) would, but that's not enough. It's not enough to focus on just investment options! Remember, Wealth Management is about more than just Investment Consulting.

What it comes down to inside of an IRA, the mistake that I see many times is that you have been steered towards mutual funds and commissioned products. You've been steered towards these "products" because you normally deal with a "Financial Advisor" in the retail world. Retail organizations answer to their shareholders, so "Advisors" often have a book of products or funds that they push above all else. These investments have an internal cost that is usually quite high. Remember, this is the cost that your "Advisor" tells you that you won't ever see or notice. There are SO many other ways to get the same types of returns and investments at a FRACTION of the cost.

Once you've accumulated your wealth in retirement, you don't need to have the types of costs associated with mutual funds or other commissioned products. One of the biggest problems with IRAs is the internal costs of the investments. Investments that sounded great when you were younger haven't changed that much. You might've been working with an "advisor" who kept investing you in the same types of mutual funds, just with different names. As your "advisor" moved you from Mutual Fund to Mutual Fund, they continued to make money. The important question to ask; did you?

## Traditional IRAs Must Be Converted Eventually

This fund was great, but now I want to move you to this fund, then I'm going to move to you to this fund. It doesn't have to be that way. I have seen internal costs of an IRA range anywhere from 2% up to 3% or even higher. When you think about that money in real dollars, it is a lot of money that you pay every year, and not a lot of service to you that's provided. If you are only paying for an Investment Consultant, it is very hard to have a clear picture of your retirement.

Mutual funds offer hidden costs to you, the investor, that nobody really knew or asked about. In today's society, the secret is out about mutual funds. We all know that they're expensive. That's one of the hidden costs in an IRA. I have seen taxes on a $500,000 IRA with no Roth conversion planning, costing up to $385,000 over that person's lifetime. Could you imagine $385,000 of your hard-earned money going straight to the IRS?

The tax cost on your IRAs is usually very high. If you don't take care of this, if you don't have a plan in place, if you haven't looked at all of your options, you could end up losing a significant amount of money because it's not about investment performance. I have seen it time and time and time again. I've sat down with families, and most of the time, it's the husbands who sit down and say, "Look at this growth on my money; this performance was great! This mutual fund did wonderful for us. Look at how much money we made." Do you know what I see when you sit down in front of me and show me the "amazing", "incredible", "eye-opening" returns inside of your IRA? A tax timebomb that is eventually going to go BOOM! The more growth inside of Tax-Deferred accounts like IRA's, 401k's, etc., the bigger the rake the IRS gets to take over your wealth. Retirement is more than investment consulting.

Retirement is about the whole plan. It's about the taxes you're going to pay, the Medicare surcharges. At this point in life, it's not about gains. It's about how much money you hang on to and how much money you pay to the IRS. Most of the time, that's an eye-opening, eye-popping item that families see when we talk about IRAs, how much money from this IRA is going directly to the IRS. It's not just when they die. It's also their beneficiaries that pay more to the IRS with the new SECURE Act. They have to pay much more money than normal. The truth of the matter is your IRA is earned income. What it comes down to is most people say, "Well, I had to have an IRA because I made too much money for a Roth IRA."

This is unequivocally false. You did not have only to have an IRA. You could not contribute directly to a Roth IRA. What you could do, though, was contribute to your IRA and immediately convert some of that money to Roth IRA. You would have had to pay the taxes on it. That was the only difference. You pay the taxes on it at that time. It's called a backdoor Roth conversion. Everybody can do this. If you still have kids or grandkids that are working, make sure that they know about this.

You can contribute directly to an IRA and turn around and convert a portion of that to a Roth IRA. You have to be careful, though. This is where the importance of wealth management and planning comes into play. You have to be careful when you make those conversions because it's all taxable. If you try to convert too much, the taxes you pay on those conversions alone make it not worth doing the conversion.

You always have to speak with a tax professional before you make those kinds of changes.

**The Idea Behind the Backdoor Concept**

The idea behind contributing directly to an IRA and then converting it right away to a Roth IRA is usually a foreign concept to the families that I meet with. First, most high-income earners have been told they make too much money to have a Roth IRA. What this means is that they can't contribute directly to a Roth IRA because they make too much money. You can still have a Roth IRA; you just can't CONTRIBUTE directly to it. The C-word is important here. You can't contribute, but you can CONVERT IRA funds to Roth IRA funds. When you convert it from an IRA to a Roth IRA, you're going to pay the taxes right away. However, everything that grows from that point forward is tax-free. It's tax-free as income later on. It grows tax-free. All the gains are tax-free. The tradeoff is worth it. If somebody has 30 years left in the workforce, would you rather have that IRA accumulate and become this big tax time bomb that'll eventually go off, or would you rather have a Roth IRA where everything in there is not subject to taxation? Would you rather pay the tax on the seed or the corn?

That would be the same concept for the SEP IRA as well. A SEP IRA is usually for higher earners, people who make a lot more money. You can basically put more money away tax-deferred, more than what somebody could put into a regular IRA. You can still convert funds to a Roth inside of a SEP, even though most high earners contributing to a SEP aren't even thinking about this.

The idea with a Backdoor Roth conversion is that you can convert as long as it was earned income. You can convert funds from IRAs, 401(k), and SEP, into Roth accounts. The difference is that, rather than going into the IRA or the SEP IRA and being tax-deferred, you have to pay the taxes that year on the amount of money you convert. If you convert $40,000 to a Roth IRA, you have to add $40,000 to your income. Maybe you put in $50,000 to your IRA, 401k, SEP, and you converted $40,000 to Roth, keeping the $10,000 in the IRA, 401k, or SEP.

All of the growth inside of the Roth from that point forward is tax-free, and when you take it out, the income is tax-free.

**Taxes Must Be Paid Eventually**

The easiest way for you to understand the importance of all of this is to realize that the taxes have to be paid eventually on IRAs and 401(k)s. All you're doing with these IRAs and 401(k)s is kicking that tax bill down the road and delaying them. The longer we wait to pay the taxes, the more money we're giving to the IRS. There is no real argument to this; it is a fact of life. If we look at history, we are in one of the lowest tax environments we have ever been in. Taxes are at a discount right now, today. The longer you wait, the higher the likelihood that you will be paying more in taxes than you need to because it is very likely taxes will go up from this point. When taxes go up, the IRS is going to get a bigger cut of your wealth.

Remember, the ideas in this book are not only to be used by you, the retiree. I love it when my readers share this information with their children and grandchildren. Backdoor conversion, for instance, is a great strategy for younger workers. Retirees who are reading this and have 401(k)s and IRAs, that money, while it sits in your 401(k) and IRA, is still considered earned income. Many of the retiree families we work with don't think that they can open a Roth IRA because you have to fund a Roth IRA with earned income, but guess what!? You can CONVERT as much or as little as you want from your IRA's and 401k's into Roth.

**No Job? You Can Still Have a Roth**

If you don't have a job, how can they have a Roth? Both 401(k)s and IRAs are earned income that you have not paid the taxes on yet. All the IRS cares about is getting their tax money. If you pay it now, you win!! You are getting to pay those taxes at a discount. The IRS would love it if you wait and tax rates go up. You are perfectly within your rights to take funds from an already established IRA or a 401(k) and convert those funds to Roth. For many people, it is a great idea to do this because the longer the money sits in the IRA or the

401(k), the higher the tax bill will be down the road. The best course of action for the families that we serve is to look at their IRAs, their 401(k)s and understand that they can still have a Roth IRA. You can do the same!

You can create a Roth IRA and fund it from your current IRA or 401(k) and potentially save yourself hundreds of thousands of dollars in taxes down the road. Many people don't know or haven't heard about this because other advisors or investment consultants don't talk about it. They aren't qualified to talk about taxes, and really there's no way for them to make money. If they're already managing funds for their clients, it's more work for them to take those funds, create a new Roth IRA, transfer funds over, invest it accordingly. It creates more work that they're not getting paid for. It's an extra step that they don't necessarily have to take, so they don't talk about it. These advisors will say, "We don't give tax advice. You'll have to go to a CPA or an Accountant for that."

Does it make sense to go to a CPA who doesn't work with your advisor? Someone who has no idea what your investment situation looks like or what the plan is? Then you're asking the CPA about Roth conversions? Well, the job of CPAs and tax professionals is to put their heads down, get to work, and look at that specific year. They try and save you the most money possible on your taxes for that year. They try and get you the most in deductions for that year. They're not looking 5 or 10 years into the future to determine the amount of money you will owe the IRS on your IRA's and 401k's. That's not their job. Their job is to go one year at a time, focus on that year, and get you the biggest amount of deductions they can.

It's so important with our families that we work with to include advanced tax planning with professionals that work directly on our team of professionals that we have vetted. Because they are retired, the runway is much shorter now, and the margin of error is minuscule. They don't have as much time. Everything has to be looked at. We can't look at this one year at a time anymore, and neither can you. That's normally what happens with all 401(k)s, all of the IRAs. Everything has been investment-related only, "We're going to grow your money, grow your money, grow your money.", but you don't get a plan on how to spend it or how much in taxes it is going to cost you!

When does the accumulation mode and mentality stop? How much is that accumulation mentality going to end up costing you? People look at me funny sometimes because that is the opposite of what most people in the financial world discuss. Normally all they do is talk about accumulation and making people money. I've sat down with families who have $15 million, $20 million in IRAs, and I've told them, "These double-digit returns are killing you right now." They always look at me strangely and ask me why. My response; "because you're making so much money, most of it is going to go to the IRS." They've had no training on Roth. They don't care about the taxes because it's never been explained to them. It's very important to remember your 401(k)s and IRAs and all of these hidden costs. You're making a lot of mistakes by not looking at taxes, by not having the right wealth management team, and those mistakes can potentially cost you hundreds of thousands of dollars.

If you don't care about yourself, remember that it's going to potentially cost your family members hundreds of thousands of dollars. The IRS is going to get their share. They always do. It's never talked about, and it is finally time that the curtain gets pulled to the side, and everybody sees what's going on with 401(k)s and IRAs.

# Chapter Four
# How the IRS Legally Double Dips on Your IRA

How does the new SECURE Act potentially double the tax to your 401(k) and IRA and allow the IRS to double-dip on the amount they can take?

The new SECURE Act has mandated that, when you have an IRA, pass away and leave that money to your children or other beneficiaries, they only have ten years to take that money out of the IRA. Before the SECURE Act, they were able to spread out those distributions from those IRAs throughout their entire lives. They could spread it out over 30, 40, even 50 years. With the new SECURE Act, those beneficiaries only have ten years to take out those funds.

Let me give you an example of this. I had a family where both of the family members passed away, and they had three children. Their IRA, when they passed away, was over $3 million. What ended up happening was those children, rather than having to take out $40,000 a year to satisfy the IRS and add the $40,000 to their income, now they have to take out $142,000 a year each to satisfy the IRS. They have to take out $142,000 the first year, but because the amount of money was so big, the money kept growing, and the next year, they each had to take out $152,000. Here's what happens. The IRS is getting a bigger chunk from the people who died. You DIED, and the IRS is still getting more of your money. Most of you are going to say, "I don't care. I'm dead." I get that, but do you really want the IRS to get more of your money than they should? Do you want them to get more of your children's money than they should?

Not only did they get more money from you when you were dead, but your family suffers too because now it has to be taken out sooner, creating a bigger tax liability for THEM. Most of you have done a good job. Your family's off the payroll. The kids are successful. You have grandkids, and they have successful careers. A lot of them are probably making six-figure incomes. Now they have to add another six-figure income to their tax situation. If they make $120,000 a year and they have to add that $142,000 that they took in distribution to their income, now they're at the top of the tax bracket. That's how the IRS double dips; they get more of your money and more of theirs because they are now paying taxes on your distribution at the highest rate (even though you are dead) and paying taxes on their OWN income at the highest rate because your IRA distributions pushed them into that higher tax bracket. The IRS wins and continues to take a rake over your wealth.

## How Can This Be Avoided?

The best way to avoid this happening is to look at those funds before you die and develop a plan. I want to stress it again: It doesn't matter how old you are; taxes are at a discount right now. You could be 80 years old and reading this book, and if you did Roth conversions at 80, it would still end up saving your beneficiaries money. Every conversion you make saves you money and saves your beneficiaries money.

You avoid that double taxing by putting a plan together with a professional wealth manager. Somebody who has the right team of individuals to look at the tax implications, to look at the investment implications, and you create a plan that will allow you to convert that IRA, that 401(k), to a Roth IRA. You have to convert it. When you get it converted, the government has no claim on that money, and the IRS has no claim on that money because you have already paid them their taxes, likely at a MUCH lower rate than what the future holds.

If there's one thing you can take from this chapter, it's this; when you leave your family members a Roth IRA, that money is completely tax-free to them. That is how you avoid unjust taxation and how you avoid the IRS double-dipping on you and your family. You pay the taxes now. You write the check now, when taxes are at a discount. You avoid the IRS getting that double-dip. You will avoid all of it.

**Convert Over Time**

I talked a little bit about the family members who had to take out that $142,000 because they couldn't stretch it out over their own lifetime thanks to the Secure Act. Let me give you another example. I worked with a family who did conversions and had over $5 million in their IRA. They converted over ten years because they were 62 when they retired. They had ten years to convert it all, but they had no income. Converting everything put them in a much lower tax bracket than they would have been if they took their RMD and had an extremely high income coming in when they were 72. They converted all $5 million, which ended up saving them, based on today's tax rates, over $3.7 million that would have gone to the IRS.

It's painful when you have to write a check right now to the IRS, but I always say it the same way. I'm someone who loves a good deal, especially on my wardrobe. I'm on Men's Warehouse and Jos. A. Bank websites all the time, looking for a good deal. I'll sit in front of my computer in the afternoon, and I'll say, "Huh, I got an email. This sports jacket is nice; I like it." Of course, like everyone else, I have to go home and check with my wife and say, "Honey, I like this jacket. What do you think?" When I get home, if the jacket was $98 when I was sitting in my chair at the office, and it's now six o'clock at night, the sale might have ended! Now the jacket is back to being $250 again. I lost the deal, and I get so upset.

If you are reading this chapter, you can relate to that in some way. You have missed out on some kind of a deal in your life. Do not let taxes be one of the biggest deals that you ever miss out on! If you wait because you're uncomfortable with this, because it's not something you've heard of before, it is going to cost you more in taxes than you can imagine. Paying three million in taxes now is better than paying six or seven million later on. You're going to sit back and say, "Wow, I let that deal go. I should have looked into this. I should have done something about it." Imagine missing out on millions of dollars because you were uncomfortable with a new strategy, or you were afraid to learn something new? Or even worse, imagine losing millions because you are just too stubborn or proud, or too much of a know it all? How would it make you feel to miss out on saving millions of dollars in retirement?

You know it's going to hurt to write the check. I know it's going to hurt, but YOU can pick how much you want it to hurt. The pain could kill you later on, or it's could hurt a little now. Which way would you like it? Because one way or another, it is going to happen. You are going to pay those taxes.

**What You Can Do Right Now**

What I want you to do right now is take a look at your current tax bracket you're in. If you don't know your current tax bracket, you have a problem in retirement right now. Take a look at what your tax bracket is right now or the dollar amount you're paying in taxes on your income. I want you to take a look at it, and I want you to think about adding even more income. You're going to have to add more income from your IRAs. Let's imagine you're adding another $50,000 a year in income from your IRAs. How does that affect your tax bracket right now? How much more are you paying right now by adding that income? Now imagine how much MORE you are going to be paying if taxes go up.

Now, I want you to do something drastic because I truly believe this is where we're headed. I want you to take those numbers, the taxes you're paying on those numbers right now, and I want you to double that tax number you're going to have to pay. If you're paying 28% or 32%, I want you to double it. Everybody looks at me like I'm crazy, but the reality is if we think back, there are certain times in this country, like in the 1970s, when the effective tax rate was 70% on anything above $200,000. Am I that crazy by saying tax rates could double? The '70s weren't that long ago.

# Chapter Five
# Freedom from Exorbitant Medicare Surcharges

When we talk about Medicare surcharges, it's important to understand the reason that people pay more. The first thing you need to know about Medicare surcharges is that Medicare costs themselves could potentially go up about 5% for the next five or six years. If you think about what you're paying for Medicare A, Medicare B, how much has it increased already from when you started? Most of you will see that there's going to be some increase. What ends up happening?

**Medicare Surcharges**

It's very easy to understand why Medicare surcharges happen. Everybody has to pay for medicare. The charges come right out of Social Security, out of your check every month. For your Medicare B premiums, if you are an individual making $87,000 or less, or if you're a married couple making $174,000 or less, you only pay around $144.60 a month at the time of this writing. Again, these numbers are usually scheduled to increase each year.

I see so much of it. I represent families that have done a very good job at preparing for retirement. When they get to retirement, they realize that they needed a specialist, a team, because having a high income in retirement ends up causing Medicare to increase.

Every time you make more, the cost of your Medicare B premiums goes up. The next step is somebody who makes above $174,000, and they're paying $202.40 per month each. It keeps going up from there. We've seen families who end up paying $462.70 per person for their Medicare B surcharges, but their next-door neighbor is still paying only $144.60.

Also, when your Medicare B premiums go up, your Medicare D premiums go up as well. Medicare D is for your prescription medications. Plans range from $12 a month up to $70 a month per person. When we add all of this up, I've seen and worked with individuals who have paid $564 per month per person when everybody else pays $177.34 per person. That amounts to almost $10,000 more per year that these families pay.

How many years do you have in retirement? Ask yourself that right now because if you have another 25 years of retirement, that's $250,000 more in Medicare premiums that you're going to pay per couple compared to a normal couple. Think about that for a minute: $250,000. Imagine 250,000 of your money…..gone.

**Why Don't Retirees Know About This?**

You are more than likely not aware of this. Most people aren't because a financial consultant or a financial advisor will not talk to you about Medicare. They're going to assume that you're going to talk to a Medicare salesperson for Medicare. That's not even correct, either, because when you go to talk to somebody about Medicare, you're usually talking to somebody about a Medicare supplement. A supplement is an addition to your Medicare B surcharges. The reason people don't hear about this is they don't work with an effective Wealth Management team. They don't work with people who look at the entire costs of retirement, not just the investments. This is very real. This happens every day.

Most of you reading this book can look right now at your Social Security statement, your check that you get every month, and you can see how much is being taken out. If there's more than $144 taken out, you have a problem that nobody has talked to you about, and most of the time, nobody is going to talk to you about it because there's no money to be made in it. There's no money to be made in helping you with your Medicare surcharges.

**My Encouragement to You**

I would encourage you to look at your Social Security statements right now and figure out exactly how much you are paying in Medicare for you and your spouse. That is unequivocally one of the best things you can do for yourself after reading this chapter. I've sat down with families who had no idea that they were paying more than they should have. That's exactly the way the Social Security administration likes it.

Why would you question it? If you're suddenly paying $300+ a month, how are you to know any different? How are you to know that somebody else is only paying $144?

That's why it's so important for you to look at this, to digest it, and to understand exactly what your cost is. Once you understand exactly what the cost is, that's when you can put the work in. That's when you can make sure you get back into that $144 tax bracket. It's as easy as being poor on paper. With the right wealth management team, you can do that. You can be poor on paper and back to paying $144 a month. You can potentially save yourself 300-500,000 dollars in needless medicare surcharges!

# Chapter Six
# IRA and 401(k) Mistakes to Avoid

Diving into this investment consultant role, it's only a portion of what I do for my families. I don't call myself a financial advisor. That makes me cringe, but I will tell you why you can't trust your investment consultant to help you with IRA 401(k) conversions to Roth IRAs. Investment consultants spend most of their time trying to figure out how you can accumulate more wealth. They are not tax professionals. They do not do taxes. They do not file taxes. This is something completely different. It's somebody else's job.

It's like asking your nurse practitioner to fix your broken bone. If you go to the doctor with your bone sticking out of your leg, you're not going to tell your doctor to fix it. Your doctor's going to send you to an orthopedic surgeon, a specialist. If your doctor does his job correctly, he's going to look at you and say, "Holy crap, your bone is sticking out of your leg! I have to send you to somebody." They're not going to try and do it themselves. It's the same thing with financial consultants. Financial consultants are not tax specialists. They don't know how to advise you on that cost and tell you how much you should do. Their job is to accumulate your money.

Let's talk about their job and what you're paying them for. The term "fiduciary" is tossed around quite a bit. Fiduciary means that your investment consultant is supposed to be putting your financial needs above their own at all costs. Here's what I always say about this: We live in an investment world where there are insurance options, there are investment options, there are all of these options out there. You are the consumer. You are the person who has these problems. You are right in the middle of that war.

You have one side over here saying, "Look at these insurance products. The market is dangerous. You want to be safe. It's retirement." You have the other side over there saying, "Oh, no, don't worry about that. You don't need insurance products. invest your money, and you'll grow it back; there's not that much risk." The fact of the matter is that the insurance world is right, and the investment world is right. The problem is you don't have professionals who take it seriously enough to dip themselves into each world.

A true fiduciary will do that. The minute you see somebody up on their soapbox on TV saying, "We don't do insurance products. We don't make investments. We don't do this. We don't do that," and start to bash that world, then you know they don't do everything. In retirement, you need someone who does everything.

We need to discuss retail versus institutional. If you already work with Fidelity or Merrill Lynch, Morgan Stanley, one of those big firms, is retail firms. Their job is to help you accumulate your wealth, and they have a certain menu that's available for you to do that.

They have certain things that they sell more of. Edward Jones sells a lot of mutual funds. There are certain things that people are comfortable with that they help their clients with. They do a good job, but the reality is when we get to retirement, we can't have one way that you do it anymore. You have to have the entire scope of the investment world open to you, whether that's investments themselves, insurance products, CDs, or whatever it is that gets you to where you need to be. That's being a true fiduciary: offering anything that the client needs for their pay.

Quite often, in retirement, we're not getting any of that advice. We're getting the same advice: "Well, let's stick with this mutual fund. Let's stick with this investment. Let's do this." You don't have this institutional view. There's a big difference between being retail and being institutional. Institutional takes you directly to the money managers. If you want a certain sector, you go directly to them. You don't have to worry about buying certain stocks. There's no more internal buying and selling. It's institutional. You're brought directly into the institution.

Families spend more of their hard-earned money when inside their IRAs and 401(k)s, they're paying close to 2%, and they're not getting any of this service or education. Listen, I don't want to clean my pool. I don't want to cut my lawn. I'm sorry. I'm not into that. I want to spend more time with my family. I want to take my kids to Disney as much as possible, so I pay people to do what I don't want to do. The difference is I pay people a reasonable amount in retirement. If working with an investment consultant who has not talked about anything in this book, you are paying too much.

**Creating a Tax Bomb**

I sat down with a family with one of those big firms that you see on television, and I'm not going to say who, but they paid one fee for their investment. They did very well for themselves. The firm did a great job of accumulating their investments, but what's one of the things that I already talked about? In retirement, returns become less important than the entire picture because as good as those returns were, that's more taxes that needed to be paid. It added to that tax time bomb before it goes off.

When we sat down with them, they realized that we could do all the same things investment-related that was happening with the current firm that they were with.

We are structured very similarly with that big-name firm on television. The difference is they could also talk to us and ask us about Roth conversions and not have us tell them, like the big firm did, "Well, you have to talk to a CPA about that. We don't give tax advice." This family had the right idea: "We're accumulating a lot of this wealth. It's all in our IRA. Should we be doing some Roth conversions so that we don't have to worry so much about these taxes?" They were not getting that service, but with us, they did get that service. They were able to convert and save themselves. Again, every time you convert, you could potentially save yourself hundreds of thousands of dollars in taxes. It's that simple.

Any investment inside your IRAs and 401(k)s, a great majority of the time, there is an internal cost for your investment. That is on top of what you're paying your advisor for their fee. If you're paying your advisor 1.25%, and your investment cost is 0.5%, you're paying 1.75%.

Most of the time, in retirement, those investments are the ones that you don't need anymore anyway. Those are the ones you can do for a fraction of the cost. It's the same investment for a fraction of the internal cost as what you're paying now. That's one of the biggest mistakes that I see in IRAs and 401(k)s, people remaining invested in investments that charge three times more than something else they could invest in it that does the same thing.

**For Younger Generations**

My advice for the younger generation is to contribute whatever your company is matching you. If your company matches you 3% or 5%, contribute that amount from your paycheck because you want that match. That is free money. Even though it's growing with taxes, it's still free money that you're getting. Anything above and beyond that, I would recommend you put as much as you can in a Roth. That would be my advice. Then, the younger generation wakes up one day, and they potentially have $200, $300, $400,000 tax-free in a Roth that they can draw from.

Even if they're 50, it doesn't matter. They still might have 15 more years to get the money in that Roth. It doesn't matter how old you are. Put as much as you can, as early as you can, into the Roth.

I had a teacher when I was 18. I don't know if he's still alive, but his name was Mr. Pogel. He was also the football coach at Niagara Wheatfield High School, where I graduated. He did a class in 2000, so this was 21 years ago now. In this class, he told us about the Roth IRA. He told all of us, "Listen, forget your graduation gifts." Back in the day, you used to have to take an economics class before you graduated. Back then, we needed to learn a little bit about the financial world before we graduated.

He would tell us, "Forget graduation presents. You need to get your family to contribute to a Roth IRA for you." He had it all broken down for us. He showed us, by starting with what we probably would have gotten for graduation money, we could have all potentially been millionaires by the time we were in our 40s, based on having that money in that Roth and letting it grow.

It was such a great lesson. Of course, none of us listened, but I think of him all the time when I talk about Roth IRAs now. I was too late. I could have potentially been a millionaire well before now. I wasn't because I didn't listen. He was saying all the right things. If he is reading this, thanks, Mr. Pogel. I did learn a lesson. I learned it a little bit late, as usual, but I learned it.

# Chapter Seven
# Exposing the Lie: Success Stories

I have countless families, and I have tons of stories. I think part of what I like the most about what I do is the ability to help people, but you have to help people who want the help. Unfortunately, I've seen people in families who were too proud, do-it-yourselfers. They don't need any help. "We know what that tax liability is going to end up being." They probably didn't, but even if they did, these types of families don't want any help.

In some of my favorite moments, I've worked with families who have had government jobs. We're talking about the hard government jobs, DEA, FBI, the jobs that were incredibly hard. They were out there putting their lives on the line, and they had no guidance whatsoever. When they retired, it was like, "Okay, I have all this money, and I have no idea what to do."

They knew right away that they needed help. I'm thinking to myself, "I've got it made. I get to help people all day long. When these people help people, they're seeing them on their worst days. They're stopping drugs from entering this country." It was my pleasure to help them. I sat down with them, and I showed them exactly, to the dollar, what the tax amount on their retirement fund was, based on today's tax rates, and then I showed them what it could end up being based on tax rates doubling by the time they are older.

Because they were younger, it could double. I made no secret about that. I always remember the looks on faces when the light bulb goes off, and families say, "Man, we have to do something about this." When people realize that it's not about the gains anymore, it's about protecting what you have, not letting the IRS take this huge rake over your wealth, freedom from unjust taxation and litigation, those are some of my favorite families to work with.

**Estate Planning**

I love when I sit down with families, and we talk about investments, Roth conversions, and Medicare surcharges. I love it just as much when we talk about estate planning. For some of these families, nobody ever told them, "Hey, listen; we should look at your will, your trust, your healthcare proxies, your power of attorney." Some of these people don't have that, and even if they do, it's not included in the overall plan. It is literally one of the most important pieces in true Wealth Management.

If I could say one thing about the importance of this, whether you sit down with me or anybody else, you must get at least your healthcare directives/proxies done. It would be best if you got your powers of attorney done. Your wills and your trusts are important, especially if you have a lot of wealth and you've done a great job-saving. I have seen too many times when a spouse could not access money or make decisions because the proper documents were not provided.

That's what's so important about the lie. The lie that you've heard your entire life is you're going to be fine in retirement. That's made most of us sleep comfy and cozy at night. The time to realize the truth is now. You're not going to be fine without the proper planning, whether you choose to admit that or not.

My grandfather was an Italian immigrant who came to this country with about $4 in his pocket. He didn't speak English that well. I wish I would have learned Italian. He died when I was 4, but he was one of my favorite people in the world. He used to say, "Adam, you can drag the jackass to the water, but you can't make him drink." You have to imagine hearing it with a VERY thick Italian accent.

He's right. If you choose to be the jackass in your story, that's fine, but this information is important to many people. That's why I chose this platform to share it. I want people to have the information because I could tell thousands of stories, but the best part of every story ends with that look in those families' eyes, that light bulb going off when they realize, "Why should I have to pay this much money? Why didn't anybody ever tell me about this?

# Chapter Eight
# Questions You Should be Asking

Right now, I want to give all of you a little bit of homework. Here are the questions that you should be asking right now in retirement. Feel free to ask your advisor because I'm telling you exactly what's going to happen. I've seen it happen more times than I care to admit, but here's exactly what's going to happen. You're going to take the information that you've learned today, and you're going to go back to the same person who hasn't given you this information, and you're asking yourselves, "Why haven't I heard this?" You're going to take this information back to them, and you're going to say, "I read this book," or you're going to show this book to them. You're going to say, "Look at all these tips in here. Look at all these items that we don't talk about. What do you think about this?"

I'm going to tell you exactly what's going to happen. That advisor is going to say to you,

"Yeah, I can do all of this." A couple of months will go by, and you'll realize that none of this is being done. Even if they do offer to do it for you, they're more than likely not the right professional, or they probably don't have the right professional team behind them to help you do it. Remember, they are Investment Consultants.

I want to stress to you that this is something we do every day. Every day when I head to the office, my team and I are doing this and only this. I only work with people close to or who are in retirement, and I do that for a reason. It's what I am good at. It's what my team is good at. What your "advisor" is good at is accumulating your money. Whether you like to admit it or not, that relationship has probably run its course because you don't need to worry about accumulating your money anymore. Now you have to worry about protecting it, about planning, about what retirement could potentially end up costing you, and how to avoid it.

I'm sorry to be the one to tell you that, but it's the reality. If you do some self-discovery and self-examination right now, imagine your situation and how it is affected by everything I have talked to you about on these pages. Imagine your life without the knowledge and truth you have read on these pages. How much does that cost? The hardest question is WHY have you not heard about these strategies? Why does it take you going to your "Financial Advisor" to get these answers? Think about it, and you know, deep down, that investment consultant relationship has probably run its course. It doesn't mean that you have to be enemies. It doesn't mean that they haven't done a great job for you up to this point. It means that this is your stop, and it's time to get off.

**Questions You Need to Ask Your Advisor**

You need to ask your advisor, "How much am I going to pay to the IRS from these 401(k)s or IRAs?" Based on today's rates, our experience has been (as of the day this book was written in 2021) many families who have a $500,000 IRA are potentially paying $300,000 plus on that amount of money to the IRS over their lifetime and their beneficiaries' lifetimes. Your beneficiaries are adding it to their income as well, so they're paying even more taxes on their income.

You also need to ask, "How much in Medicare surcharges am I going to pay from 65 on?" You need to ask that question. You will be very hard-pressed to find people who will give you that answer, but you still need to ask that question. You need something in your hand that shows you exactly how much you're going to pay if you do nothing.

You also need to ask hard questions. "What are my fees right now?" Of course, whoever you're working with is going to say, "Well, I charge you 1%," or, "I charge you 1.25%." That's not what I'm talking about. I'm talking about your investments specifically. How much are you paying internally for your investments? Is it 1.25%, and then your investments' internal costs are another half or three-quarters of a percent? If so, you're paying too much for the service you are probably receiving.

You need to ask yourself, "What's important about my legacy? What is important about my retirement right now? What have I accomplished? What do I still want to accomplish?" These are the hard questions. These are the questions you don't ask yourself because you've been head down, grinding away and working your entire career, accumulating your wealth for this moment. You knew you had to save as much money as possible for retirement. My question to you is, "now what?" You've retired, now what? And that's one of the hardest questions that only you can answer. You have to answer it. Your retirement is about the lifestyle you want and the one you can pay for.

You have to face it; you have to know what you're "why" is for right now, for retirement. You have to know what you still want to accomplish, what goals you want to achieve, what legacy you want to leave for your family. You need to answer all of those questions, and you're not going to get that answer from an investment consultant. You are not going to get that answer from me. YOU are the only one that can provide that answer.

## Questions to Ask Yourself

Some of the other questions you need to ask yourself are, "Where are my investments now? What are they invested in?" You have no idea how many times I pull back the curtain, and I show families exactly what they're invested in, exactly what the cost is, and it doesn't come down to cost at all. They're invested in a way that doesn't line up with their religious views or their fundamental morals or values. They say, "Why am I invested in this? I don't even believe in this." That has happened so many more times than I like to count, but it's something that not a lot of people think about. When you were younger, you didn't necessarily have the same values that you have today. Your investments need to match your values.

The other question that you need to ask is, "Where am I going? What am I going to do? How do I want to get there?" Those are hard questions as well. I can show you exactly how much money you can save, exactly how much your Medicare surcharges are going to be. I can show you exactly how your lifestyle will look, your estate planning, your taxes. It can all be done for you, but if you don't have a clear direction of where you want to go, all of that is pieces of paper on a desk.

## Finding the Answers

I would say most of the answers to these questions can only be found by you. For some of these numbers questions, the 401(k) questions, the Roth conversions, the Medicare surcharges, it's going to be hard for you to get the answers on your own.

You need to look at your social security statement because you need to know how much you're paying in Medicare right now. You need to know how much money is in your IRA. You need to know how much growth you've had for the past couple of years and the expected growth. We need to have examples of hypothetically how much it's going to grow to when it's time for you to start taking your money out when you turn 72. All of this information can be found on financial statements, and your Medicare surcharges can be found on your Social Security statements. Your income levels are one of the most important pieces of your puzzle. Your income levels can be found on your tax return. Whatever you decide to do, it's important to ask these questions.

I hope that you will take action and get the information that can potentially truly change your retirement forever and possibly save you millions. You need the answers to these hard questions. You need to ask them now because you don't want three years from now to realize you're not going to make it through retirement living the lifestyle you want. What's most important to me is that you have a retirement of significance.

# Chapter Nine
# Here's How We Can Help You

Every time I meet with somebody for the first time, my team and I generate two reports for them. We generate a Medicare surcharge analysis that shows you exactly how much in Medicare surcharges that you could potentially pay if you do nothing. We also prepare a Roth conversion analysis that shows you exactly how much money you have in IRAs and 401(k)s and how much of that money will end up going to the IRS.

Of course, that's all based on today's tax rates. I want to stress one more time that you're in the lowest tax environment in over 40 years. To help people and give them those reports, we go through a whole list of questions when we sit down with them. It's not questions about finances. It's questions like we've discussed on these pages. Where are you going, and what are you hoping to accomplish? What does that look like? How much does it cost?

It's about getting together and seeing if my team and I can bring any real value to those families. We certainly do not work with all families that come into our office. What we will do, though, is sit down with you, assess your situation, and tell you what we feel is the best way for you to move forward to make your retirement even better. If we can't help you, we always refer you to someone who can. You will always get the answers when you sit in the chairs in front of us. That's what people need more than anything: the answers. I say that because sometimes you're not going to like the answers, but I will never sugarcoat it. We will never beat around the bush. We will always give you a true fiduciary opinion about the way your situation looks right now. We will give you numerical facts about how it's going to look in the future.

By the end of the first meeting, you'll feel completely confident and comfortable, knowing that you're going to have the answers when we deliver those reports to you. You're going to know exactly how much your Medicare surcharges could cost you, how much not doing any Roth conversions could cost you, and how much taxes you'll have to pay for Roth conversions. What's the right conversion number for your scenario? You'll have a lot of those answers the second time we meet. You'll have two reports that show you those numbers.

I hope by now that you've realized you have done a tremendous job of getting to this point in your retirement. My job is to help it become even better for you. You are at a point now where a transition is needed. This is uncharted territory, and quite frankly, it's dangerous territory. Our job, and that of any real Wealth Manager, is to take what you have done and help it become even better for you, to help your retirement become even more efficient, to help you sleep even better at night. That's our primary role. It's not growing your money and returns and dividends. It's helping your retirement become one of significance.

## Exposing the Lie! Discover the "Actual" Cost of Your Retirement…

It's nice to know you did everything you were supposed to do to ensure you and your family can enjoy your retirement. You saved and put away faithfully. You may have even put extra money into your 401(k) and IRA.

Imagine knowing exactly how you can start taking income from your investments and how you can pay the least amount of taxes legally allowed! Wouldn't it be great to know exactly how much retirement is going to cost you? Imagine finally getting those answers, finally understanding how this is all supposed to work!

I help people like you in retirement by eliminating needless Medicare surcharges that could cost hundreds of thousands of dollars. I make sure you don't lose large amounts of your wealth to taxes and the IRS. You can have a retirement of real significance just knowing how to implement what is being discussed in this book!

To learn more about the ideas in this book, here's what you do next.

Step 1: Download our latest Retirement Evolved reports, including **"The Roth Decision, 12 Reasons Why You Should Go Roth"** Your email will ensure that you receive all of our reports as they are published, absolutely free of charge. Just head to our landing page below:

www.taxfreefortmyers.com

Step 2: Register for our latest webinar, **"Taxes and Retirement"** at our official landing page:

www.taxfreefortmyers.com

Step 3: Schedule a 45-minute **Strategy Session** where we create a personalized Roth Analysis and Medicare Surcharge Report.

To book a meeting on Calendly or to speak with Adam directly, email **adam@evolveswfl.com**

Made in the USA
Middletown, DE
04 February 2024